*Simply* COLOR

# PURPLE

*Simply* COLOR

# PURPLE

## A Crayon Box for Quilters

**VANESSA CHRISTENSON**
*of V & Co.*

Published in 2015 by Lucky Spool Media, LLC
www.luckyspool.com
info@luckyspool.com

**Text** © Vanessa Christenson
**Editor** Susanne Woods
**Designer** Kristy Zacharias
**Based on the design by** Rae Ann Spitzenberger
**Illustrations** Kari Vojtechovsky
**Photographer** © Lauren Hunt, except where noted

The information in this book is accurate and complete to the best of our knowledge. All recommendations are made without guarantee on the part of the author or Lucky Spool Media, LLC. The author and publisher disclaim any liability in connection with this information.

Photograph pages 86, 106 and 107 © Vanessa Christenson

9 8 7 6 5 4 3 2 1

First Edition
Printed in China

Library of Congress Cataloging-in-Publication Data available upon request

ISBN 978-1-940655-13-0

LSID0021

*To my family who
supports me and loves
me unconditionally.*

# CONTENTS

## *The* PROJECTS

# WELCOME TO
# *Simply* COLOR

As a fabric designer I have to illustrate how a whole slew of colors go well together, and explain why the shade or hues in the line were picked. Before I became a fabric designer, most of my quilts focused on one to four colors. I believe there is beauty in each color and I love how different hues or shades can create a simple but elegant look when you focus on each individual color. All people view color differently our interpretation of color depends on light and the interplay of adjacent colors and textures. In this book we will explore different shades of purple and some colors that go well with purple.

## ABOUT THIS BOOK

Throughout you will notice some common terms and abbreviations used in sewing (for example, WOF is used for "width of fabric," meaning the measurement of the fabric from selvage to selvage). Another basic in quilt making is that the most common seam allowance is one quarter of an inch (or ¼").

Every quilt maker, beginner or experienced, starts the same way: picking out fabric, cutting it up, and putting it back together again to create a beautiful and loved quilt. If you are a beginner, the Lucky Spool website has a wonderful free downloadable PDF of quilt making basics that is a great place to start your journey.

I find beauty in the simplicity of color. I hope that I can inspire you to find that beauty as well.

## COLOR THEORY
## OF PURPLE

Every color creates a mood and inspires emotions within us. Although how color impacts our senses and feelings can morph over time, it often has the ability to evoke strong responses.

The word "purple" is commonly used to cover the range of colors that fall into the segment denoted as "violet" in the visible light spectrum. These colors are at that end of the visible spectrum that has the shortest wavelength. Ultraviolet light which is invisible to the human eye, has the next shortest wavelength. Thus, the shortest wavelengths of violet which are next to ultraviolet, seem dark and somewhat dull to the human eye. This makes it difficult for us to discriminate between the cooler and warmer hues. Purples, at slightly longer wavelengths, are easier for us to see and have a richer range of color. "Purple" has therefore become the generic name when referring to the color of fabrics, dyes, cloths and cottons. As distinct from "spectral" purple which is a true color, purple for dyes is made from a mixture of red and blue pigments. However, it seems to be easier for most of us to enjoy when the hues of purple are either very cool with lots of added blue or very warm with lots of added red.

The color is associated with royalty, luxury, and plenty. Purple can balance the mind and mitigate fear and is a favorite among young girls. Most cultures believe that it represents wisdom and a sense of justice and it is thought to be a color highly creative people are drawn toward.

Purple was actually one of the earliest dyes ever used, and its ancient extraction process will surprise you (see page 56)! Used extensively for celebrations by the British monarchy today, purple has long been the preferred color for the upper classes: Julius Caesar decreed that only the emperor could wear purple, and Nero took it a step further making it a crime punishable by death for anyone other than the emperor to wear it.

# THE COLOR WHEEL

The color wheel helps identify why some combinations work well and some do not. For the most part, what "works" depends on the goals of your quilt design and the effect you are trying to achieve. Understanding how to create a variety of combinations will help you use the color purple in the most effective way. The color wheel serves as a tool to help us have that conversation.

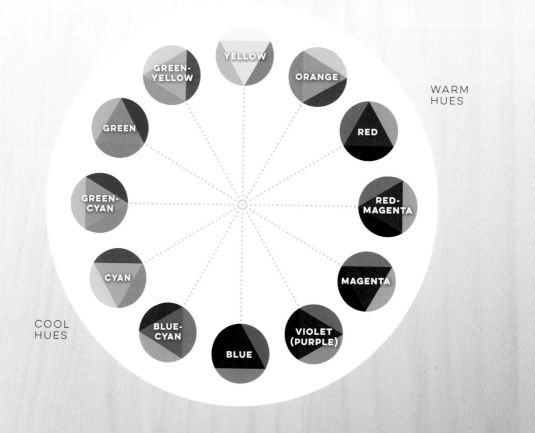

## Hues

The hue is the pure color. Each hue has many variations, from light to dark and from intense to muted. Plum and lilac are variations of the violet (purple) hue.

### *Tints*

Tints are the pure hue with added white. These will always be lighter than the pure hue and have a softer, more muted feel. They are light in color value.

## Shades

Shades are the pure hue with added black. These will always be darker than the pure hue and have a deeper, more saturated look. They are dark in color value.

## Tones

Tones are the pure hue with added gray. Tones are muddy and can vary greatly in saturation and intensity depending on the gray used.

## *Value*

Value is used to
describe how light
or dark a color is.
Light value tends to
include tints, and
dark value tends to
include shades.

## *Saturation*

Saturation is used to describe how bright a color is. Highly saturated fabrics have an almost electric quality, whereas fabrics that are low in saturation are more subtle. Another big difference between purple and violet (see page 20) is that violet can become more or less saturated (or bluer), whereas purple cannot.

## A NOTE ABOUT VIOLET

All you color theory buffs out there know that "purple" is not the correct term to use when you have a conversation about color. Whereas purple is actually a composite of red and blue, violet (the correct term) is a true spectral color with its own wavelength in the spectrum of visible light.

On the traditional color wheel, which is based on red, yellow and blue (as opposed to the CMY wheel we use here, based on cyan, magenta and yellow) both violet and purple occupy a space, with violet being closer to blue and purple being closer to red. For the purposes of this book, we acknowledge that violet is the correct term to use for both the traditional color wheel and the CMY wheel, but for the title of this book and for the projects described herein, we have chosen to use the more commonly used term — Purple.

## *Color Combinations*

Looking at the color wheel, you will see that there are many possible combinations that can complement your purple quilts. We use the CMY wheel instead of the blue, red, yellow you may be familiar with. Because the blue, red, yellow tends to skew to the warmer colors on the wheel, we find this CMY version does a better job of representing a balanced, wider range of visible colors.

My patterns tend to focus on two or three color combinations to really allow the purple to shine through, and to allow quilters to swap in any color of their choice if they want to create a different look.

## TETRAD

Tetrad is a combination that uses three additional colors that are an equal distance from each other on the wheel. For example, green/ yellow, cyan, and red form a tetrad in combination with purple.

## TRIAD

Triad is created when two additional
colors are selected that are an equal
distance from each other on the wheel.
In this case, green/cyan and orange
form a triadic combination with purple.

## COMPLEMENTARY

The complement of a color is the one located directly opposite on the color wheel. The complementary color of purple is green/yellow. Using only these two colors creates an intense combination, so when choosing fabrics, it is important to pay attention to the saturation levels.

## SPLIT COMPLEMENTARY

A split complementary color combination is made by using one color on either side of the complementary color. For purple, the split complementary would be created using green and yellow.

## DOUBLE COMPLEMENTARY

Using purple with its complementary color, green/yellow, then selecting a second complementary pair of colors equal distance from the original pair is called a double complementary. Purple with blue/cyan, green/yellow, and orange would create this combination.

## ANALOGOUS AND MONOCHROME

Working very closely within the tints and tones of one hue creates a monochromatic design, while using purple with the colors on either side of it (blue/cyan, blue, magenta and red/magenta) creates an analogous grouping.

## *Interchangeable Projects*

While it is important and inspiring to understand how purple interacts with other colors, I wanted the quilts and projects in this Simply Color series to be interchangeable both with each color in the series and within the individual books. Because of that, I use purple and one or two neutrals in many of the projects. This allows you to more easily see how swapping out just one fabric can feature your favorite color. I do hope that the Color Theory section inspires you to experiment. For example, the Grape Juice quilt (see page 88) would look great with a double complementary combination.

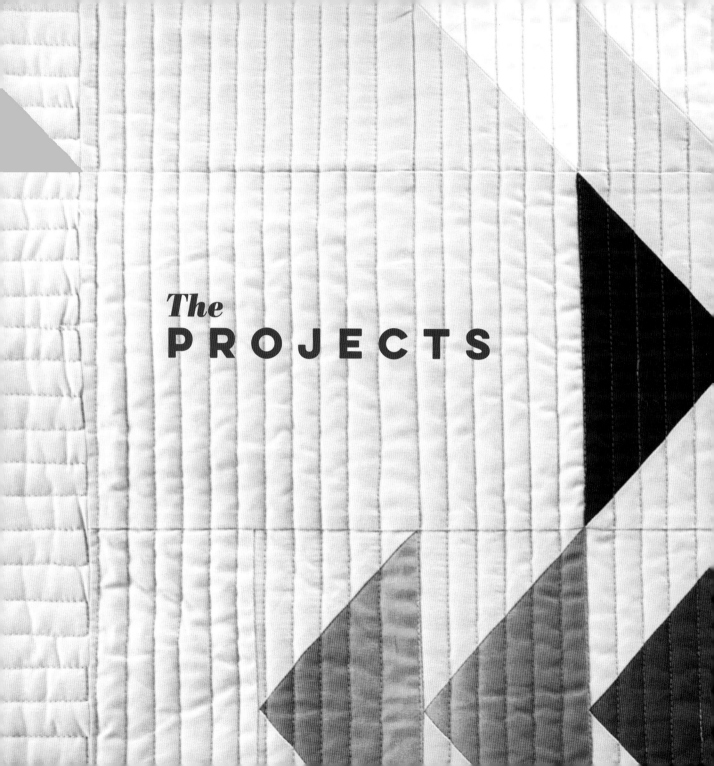

# The
# PROJECTS

*Flying*
SOUTH

*Flying geese quilts just have a simple elegance. This quilt is large with a simple design that would look great on your bed, or to take out on a beautiful summer evening as your picnic blanket with room enough for you and quite a few other family and friends.*

**Finished Quilt Size:**
84'' x 84''

**Finished Block Size:**
42'' x 42''

## Materials
**Gray Background Fabric:**
6½ yards

**Eggplant Ombré Fabric:**
1½ yards

**Gray Ombré Fabric:** ¾ yard

**Aqua Ombré Fabric:** ⅝ yard

**Backing Fabric:** 7½ yards

**Binding Fabric:** ⅝ yard

**Batting:** 90'' x 90''

**Water-soluble pen**

## Cutting

**From Background Fabric, cut:**
(28) 3½'' x WOF strips
  *Subcut (12) 3½'' squares from each strip for a total of 336 squares*
(20) 6½'' x WOF strips
  *Subcut 4 strips into (4) 30½'' x 6½'' rectangles*
  *Subcut 4 strips into (4) 24½'' x 6½'' rectangles and (12) 3½'' x 6½'' rectangles*
  *Subcut 4 strips into (4) 21½'' x 6½'' rectangles and (8) 6½'' squares*
  *Subcut 4 strips into (8) 18½'' x 6½'' rectangles*
  *Subcut 4 strips into (16) 9½'' x 6½'' rectangles*

**From Eggplant Ombré Fabric, cut:**
(8) 6½'' x WOF strips
  *Subcut (86) 3½'' x 6½'' rectangles*

**From Gray Ombré Fabric, cut:**
(4) 6½'' x WOF strips
  *Subcut (46) 3½'' x 6½'' rectangles*

**From Aqua Ombré Fabric, cut:**
(3) 6½'' x WOF strips
  *Subcut (36) 3½''x 6½'' rectangles*

**From Backing Fabric, cut:**
(3) 31'' x 90'' rectangles

**From Binding Fabric, cut:**
(9) 2½'' x WOF strips

## Making the Flying Geese

**1.** Using a water-soluble pen and a ruler, draw a line from corner to corner on the wrong sides of the 336 Background Fabric Squares. (Fig. 1)

*Figure 1*

**2.** Place a marked 3½" square on the left side of a 3½" x 6½" Ombré Rectangle (eggplant, gray, or aqua) with the drawn line visible. The drawn line should go from the top left corner to the bottom right corner of the background fabric square. (Fig. 2)

*Figure 2*

**3.** Sew on the drawn line.

**4.** Trim to the left of the sewn line, leaving a ¼" seam allowance. Press the triangle open.

**5.** Repeat for the opposite side of the rectangle. This time, the drawn diagonal line should go from the top right to the bottom left of the Background Fabric Square. Trim to the right side of the sewn line. (Fig. 3)

*Figure 3*

**6.** Repeat for all the Ombré Rectangles until you have 168 flying geese units.

*86 Eggplant*
*Flying Geese Units*

*36 Aqua*
*Flying Geese Units*

*46 Gray*
*Flying Geese Units*

## *Assembling the Rows*

**QUADRANT 1**

| | BACKGROUND RECTANGLES | EGGPLANT FLYING GEESE | AQUA FLYING GEESE | GRAY FLYING GEESE |
|---|---|---|---|---|
| Row 1 | 3½" x 6½" | 3 | | |
| | 30½" x 6½" | | | |
| Row 2 | 18½" x 6½" | | | 5 |
| | 9½" x 6½" | | | |
| Row 3 | 6½" x 6½" | 5 | | |
| | 21½" x 6½" | | | |
| Row 4 | 9½" x 6½" | 4 | 6 | |
| | 3½" x 6½" | | | |
| Row 5 | 18½" x 6½" | 5 | | |
| | 9½" x 6½" | | | |
| Row 6 | 3½" x 6½" | 3 | | 8 |
| | 6½" x 6½" | | | |
| Row 7 | 24½" x 6½" | | 3 | |
| | 9½" x 6½" | | | |

## Assembling the Rows

**1.** Following the chart (see page 39), gather supplies for each row. Label each pile to make construction easier.

**2.** Referencing Figure 4, assemble Row 1, ensuring all the points are facing to the left. Press all seams open.

**Figure 4**

**3.** Referencing Figure 5, assemble Row 2, ensuring all the points are facing to the right. Press all seams open.

**Figure 5**

**4.** Referencing Figure 6, assemble Row 3, ensuring all the points are facing to the left. Press all seams open.

**Figure 6**

**5.** Referencing Figure 7, assemble Row 4, ensuring all the points are facing to the right. Press all seams open.

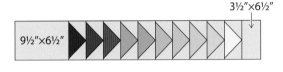

**Figure 7**

**6.** Referencing Figure 8, assemble Row 5, ensuring all the points are facing to the left. Press all seams open.

**Figure 8**

**7.** Referencing Figure 9, assemble Row 6, ensuring all the points are facing to the right. Press all seams open.

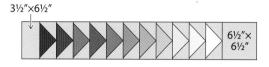

*Figure 9*

**8.** Referencing Figure 10, assemble Row 7, ensuring all the points are facing to the left. Press all seams open.

*Figure 10*

**9.** Referencing Figure 11, sew the 7 rows together. Press seams open.

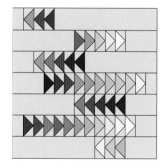

*Figure 11*

**10.** Following the remaining Quadrant charts, repeat Steps 2-9 to create a total of 4 Flying Geese Quadrants.

**QUADRANT 2**

| | BACKGROUND RECTANGLES | EGGPLANT FLYING GEESE | AQUA FLYING GEESE | GRAY FLYING GEESE |
|---|---|---|---|---|
| Row 1 | 3½'' x 6½'' | | | 3 |
| | 30½'' x 6½'' | | | |
| Row 2 | 18½'' x 6½'' | | 5 | |
| | 9½'' x 6½'' | | | |
| Row 3 | 6½'' x 6½'' | 5 | | |
| | 21½'' x 6½'' | | | |
| Row 4 | 9½'' x 6½'' | 6 | 4 | |
| | 3½'' x 6½'' | | | |
| Row 5 | 18½'' x 6½'' | 5 | | |
| | 9½'' x 6½'' | | | |
| Row 6 | 3½'' x 6½'' | 3 | | 8 |
| | 6½'' x 6½'' | | | |
| Row 7 | 24½'' x 6½'' | 3 | | |
| | 9½'' x 6½'' | | | |

## QUADRANT 3

| | BACKGROUND RECTANGLES | EGGPLANT FLYING GEESE | AQUA FLYING GEESE | GRAY FLYING GEESE |
|---|---|---|---|---|
| Row 1 | 3½" x 6½"<br>30½" x 6½" | 3 | | |
| Row 2 | 18½" x 6½"<br>9½" x 6½" | | 5 | |
| Row 3 | 6½" x 6½"<br>21½" x 6½" | | | 5 |
| Row 4 | 9½" x 6½"<br>3½" x 6½" | 4 | | 6 |
| Row 5 | 18½" x 6½"<br>9½" x 6½" | 5 | | |
| Row 6 | 3½" x 6½"<br>6½" x 6½" | 3 | 8 | |
| Row 7 | 24½" x 6½"<br>9½" x 6½" | 3 | | |

**QUADRANT 4**

| | BACKGROUND RECTANGLES | EGGPLANT FLYING GEESE | AQUA FLYING GEESE | GRAY FLYING GEESE |
|---|---|---|---|---|
| Row 1 | 3½" x 6½" | | | 3 |
| | 30½" x 6½" | | | |
| Row 2 | 18½" x 6½" | | 5 | |
| | 9½" x 6½" | | | |
| Row 3 | 6½" x 6½" | 5 | | |
| | 21½" x 6½" | | | |
| Row 4 | 9½" x 6½" | 10 | | |
| | 3½" x 6½" | | | |
| Row 5 | 18½" x 6½" | 5 | | |
| | 9½" x 6½" | | | |
| Row 6 | 3½" x 6½" | 3 | | 8 |
| | 6½" x 6½" | | | |
| Row 7 | 24½" x 6½" | 3 | | |
| | 9½" x 6½" | | | |

## Assembling the Quilt Top

**1.** Referencing Figure 12, arrange the 4 Flying Geese Quadrants into a 4-Patch, rotating the blocks so that each long string of flying geese points in a different direction.

**2.** Sew blocks into rows. Press seams open.

**3.** Sew the rows together. Press seams open.

## Finishing

**1.** Layer with batting and backing fabric, baste, and quilt as desired.

**2.** Attach binding using your favorite method.

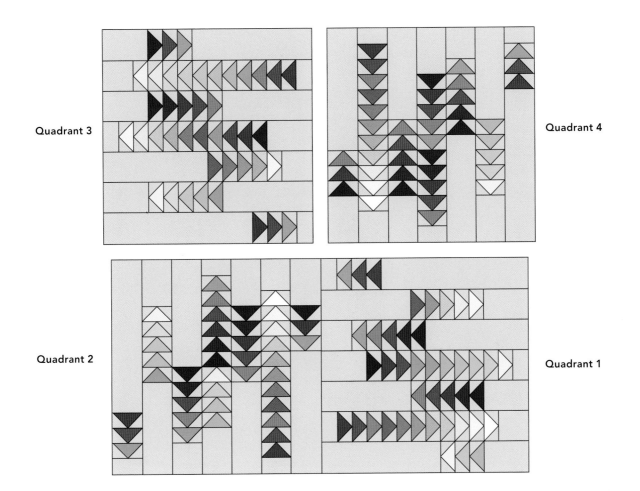

Quadrant 3

Quadrant 4

Quadrant 2

Quadrant 1

*Figure 12*

SPOOLS

**T**hread is used to mend, create, patch up and put together. Usually the person doing these things is one who loves and takes care of you. This quilt would be such a beautiful gift of appreciation to the one who has been there for you. Four spools of thread can be made in different colors or in one favorite color! Use up those scraps!

**Finished Quilt Size:**
72" x 72"

**Finished Block Size:**
36" x 36"

## Materials

**Assortment of 16 Purple Fabrics:** ¼ yard of each

**Tan Solid Fabric:** 1½ yards

**Cream/White Text Fabric:** 1⅛ yards

**Cream/Black Text Fabric:** ⅜ yard

**Backing Fabric:** 4½ yards

**Binding Fabric:** ⅝ yard

**Batting:** 78" x 78"

## Cutting

**From each Purple Fabric, cut:**

(4) 2" X WOF strips, for a total of 64 purple strips

**From Tan Fabric, cut:**

(8) 6½" x WOF strips
   Subcut (2) 6½" squares and (1) 6½" x 24" rectangle from each strip

**From Cream/White Text Fabric, cut:**

(6) 6½" x WOF strips
   Subcut (6) 6½" x 36½" rectangles

**From Cream/Black Text Fabric, cut:**

(2) 6½" x WOF strips
   Subcut (2) 6½" x 36½" rectangles

**From Backing Fabric, cut:**

(2) 40" x 78" rectangles

**From Binding Fabric, cut:**

(8) 2½" x WOF strips

## Assembling the Spool Blocks

**1.** Gather (1) 2″ x WOF strip from each of the 16 Purple Fabrics. Sew the strips together along the long edges to create a 24½″ x WOF strip set. Press seams open as you attach each strip. (Fig. 1)

**2.** Repeat to create a total of 4 purple strip sets.

**3.** Trim each strip set to 24½″ square for a total of 4 Strip Set Blocks. (Fig. 2)

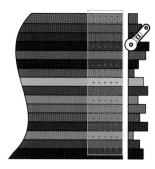

*Figure 2*

*Figure 1*

**TIP:** It doesn't matter what order you sew the strips in. I chose a scrappy style, but the decision is yours. Lay out the strips and play around with the sequence. I made each spool different. Perhaps you'd prefer to make them all the same for a more orderly look. Have fun with the possibilities!

**4.** Attach a 6½″ x 24½″ Tan strip to the top and bottom of a Strip Set Block. (Fig. 3)

*Figure 3*

**5.** Repeat to create a total of 4 Spool Centers. Set aside.

**6.** Draw a diagonal line from corner to corner on the wrong side of each of the 6½″ Tan Squares. (Fig. 4)

*Figure 4*

**7.** Place a Tan Square on top of a 6½″ x 36½″ Cream/White Text Rectangle, right sides together. The diagonal line on the Tan Square should start in the top outer corner and end at the bottom inner corner. Align the short raw edges of the Tan Square and White/Cream Text Rectangle and pin into place.

**8.** Repeat Step 7 with another Tan Square at the other end of the Cream/White Text Rectangle. Make sure the diagonal line on the Tan Square starts in the top outer corner and ends at the bottom inner corner. (Fig. 5)

*Figure 5*

**9.** Sew along the drawn lines. Trim ¼" away from each drawn line, leaving a ¼" seam allowance. You will be trimming to the left of the drawn line on the left side of the strip and to the right of the drawn line on the right side of the strip. (Fig. 6)

*Figure 6*

## THE COLOR PURPLE AND THE ANCIENT PHOENICIANS

Archaeologists discovered that as early as the 15th century BC in Phoenicia (now Lebanon) a tiny sea snail called the spiny dye-murex was used by the thousands. Mountains of these snail shells were found in the large coastal cities of Sidon and Tyre. Archaeologists have determined that these snail shells were used to create a particular shade of purple now called Tyrian purple.

These tiny predatory snails were removed from their 2″ shells and soaked until they swelled enough that a small gland could be accessed and removed. These glands were then punctured and the contents were grouped together and left in the sunlight. Over the course of many days, the color would transform from white to yellow/green, to green, to violet, to red, and finally to a particular shade of purple. Only then could this pigment be used for dyeing cloth. The dyes this slow and expensive process produced were remarkably lustrous, deep and colorfast, which soon caught the attention of the ancient noblemen.

Quickly, Tyrian purple became the color associated with royalty across the entire Mediterranean. Others tried to re-create this dye using a much less expensive combination of indigo and other plants, but those who sold this counterfeit dye were severely punished.

Eventually, various cheaper mineral based dyes were developed to satisfy the huge and lucrative demand. In the 19th Century some synthetics arrived with "mauvine" (aniline purple) and "fuchsine" (a brilliant purple) and in the 1950's we had the wonderfully light stable and color fast family of "quinacridones". We were very fortunate, since in 2008 Paul Friedander re-created the original dye — he purchased 12,000 mollusks for $3,500 that produced 1.4 ounces of dye. Enough to color a single fat quarter cut of fabric.

**10.** Press the triangle open with the seams toward the Tan fabric.

**11.** Repeat Steps 7-10 to create a total of 6 Cream/White Text Half-Square Strips.

**12.** Using the 2 Cream/Black Text 6½" x 36½" Rectangles, repeat Steps 7-10 to create a total of 2 Cream/Black Text Half-Square Strips.

**13.** Attach a Half-Square Strip to the right and left of each Spool Block. Press seams open (Fig. 7). The Cream/Black Text Half-Square Strips can be placed wherever you like to create interest (see detail photo on page 55).

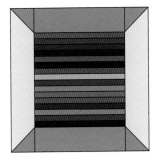

*Figure 7*

## Assembling the Quilt Top

**1.** Referencing Figure 8, arrange the completed blocks in alternating orientations.

**2.** Sew the blocks into 2 rows of 2 blocks each. Sew the rows together, maintaining the orientation of the layout. Press seams open.

## Finishing

**1.** Layer with batting and backing fabric, baste, and quilt as desired.

**2.** Attach binding using your favorite method.

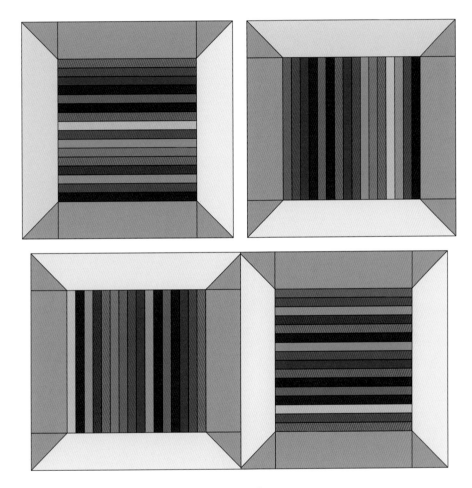

*Figure 8*

# *That's Sew Betty*

# SEWING MACHINE COVER

No one likes a dusty sewing machine. Even if you use your machine daily, most likely if its out in the open, dust will collect on it. This simple and cute sewing machine cover has pockets for weights on the corners to make it really easy to slip on and off and protect your sewing machine in between sewing sessions!

**Finished Size:** 20'' x 32'' unfolded; 20'' x 14'' x 4'' on a sewing machine

## Materials

**Dark Gray Background Fabric:** ⅝ yard

**Magenta Fabric:** 1 fat quarter OR a 12'' x 16'' piece

**Eggplant Fabric:** 4'' square

**Light Gray Fabric:** 5'' square

**Purple Backing Fabric:** ⅝ yard

**Binding Fabric:** ¼ yard

**Batting:** 20½'' x 32½''

**Water-soluble pen**

**4 small curtain weights**

## Cutting

**From Dark Gray Background Fabric, cut:**

(1) 20½'' x WOF strip

  *Subcut (1) 19½'' x 20½'' rectangle*

  *Subcut (1) 1½'' x 20½'' strip*

  *Subcut (1) 9'' x 19½'' rectangle*

    Subcut (1) 9'' x 12½'' rectangle

      Subcut (2) 4½'' x 12½'' rectangles

      Subcut (1) 5'' x 9'' rectangle, then trim to 5'' x 7½''

      Subcut (1) 2'' x 9'' strip

  *Subcut (1) 2'' x 12'' rectangle from remaining fabric*

    Subcut (1) 2'' square

    Trim remaining piece to 1½'' x 10''

      Subcut (1) 1½'' x 2½'' rectangle

      Subcut (1) 1½'' x 7½'' rectangle

**(cutting continued on page 64)**

## Cutting (continued)

**From Magenta Fabric, cut:**

(1) 11½″ x 16″ rectangle

   *Subcut (2) 11½″ x 1½″ strips*

   *Subcut (1) 11½″ x 2″ strip*

   *Subcut (1) 4½″ x 11″ rectangle*

      Subcut (1) 4½″ x 5″ rectangle

      Subcut (1) 4½″ x 3″ rectangle

      Subcut (1) 3½″ x 3″ rectangle

**From Eggplant Fabric,**
**cut:** (1) 1½″ x 2″ rectangle
(1) 1½″ x 3½″ rectangle

**From Light Gray Fabric,**
**cut:** (1) 4½″ x 3″ rectangle

**From Purple Backing Fabric,**
**cut:**

(1) 20½″ x WOF strip

   *Subcut (1) 20½″ x 32½″*
   *rectangle*

   *Subcut (4) 4″ squares from*
   *remaining fabric*

**From Binding Fabric, cut:**

(3) 2½″ x WOF strips

## Making the Sewing Machine Block

**Note:** Refer to diagram Figure 4 (see page 66) for guidance.

**1.** Working from left to right, sew the 9″ x 2″ Dark Gray Background Rectangle to the 1½″ x 2″ Eggplant Rectangle. Attach the 2″ Dark Gray Background Square to the other side of the Eggplant Rectangle. This is the Spool Strip.

**2.** Sew a 11½″ x 1½″ Magenta Strip to the bottom of the Spool Strip (Fig. 1). Set aside.

*Figure 1*

**3.** Working from left to right, sew the 3½″ x 3″ Magenta Rectangle to the 4½″ x 3″ Light Gray Rectangle. Attach the 4½″ x 3″ Magenta Rectangle to the other side of the Light Gray Rectangle. This is the Screen Strip.

**4.** Sew the Screen Strip to the bottom of the pieced unit from Step 2.

**5.** Sew the remaining 11½″ x 1½″ Magenta Strip to the bottom of the Screen Strip (Fig. 2). Set aside.

*Figure 2*

**6.** Working from left to right, sew the 7½″ x 5″ Dark Gray Background Rectangle to the 4½″ x 5″ Magenta Rectangle. This is the Throat Strip.

**7.** Sew the Throat Strip to the bottom of the pieced unit from Step 5.

**8.** Sew the 11½″ x 2″ Magenta Strip to the bottom of the pieced unit from Step 8.

**9.** This is the Machine Unit (Fig. 3). Set aside.

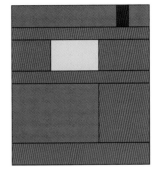

*Figure 3*

**10.** Working from bottom to top, sew the 1½″ x 7½″ Dark Gray Background Rectangle to the 1½″ x 3½″ Eggplant Rectangle. Attach the 1½″ x 2½″ Dark Gray Background Rectangle to the top of the Eggplant Rectangle. This is the 1½″ x 12½″ Wheel Strip.

**11.** Sew the Wheel Strip to the right side of the Machine Unit from Step 8. The long Dark Gray Background Strip should be at the bottom.

**12.** If necessary, trim your Sewing Machine Block to 12½'' square. (Fig. 4)

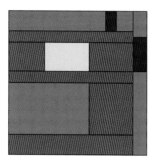

*Figure 4*

**3.** Sew the 20½'' x 19½'' Dark Gray Background Strip to the top of the unit from Step 2 to create the Pieced Cover. (Fig. 5)

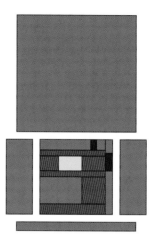

*Figure 5*

## Assembling the Panel Top

**1.** Sew (2) 4½'' x 12½'' Dark Gray Background Rectangles to the left and right sides of the Sewing Machine Block.

**2.** Sew the 20½'' x 1½'' Dark Gray Background Strip to the bottom of the unit from Step 1.

## Quilting and Finishing the Cover

**1.** Using a water-soluble pen and a ruler, draw a 1'' crosshatch design on the pieced cover.

**2.** Prepare for quilting by creating a quilt sandwich. Place the 20½″ x 32½″ piece of Purple Backing Fabric right side down. Follow with the batting and the Pieced Cover, right side up.

**3.** Baste as desired.

**4.** Set your sewing machine to a longer-than-usual stitch length (approximately 4.0 mm). Sew on the drawn crosshatch lines to create the Quilted Cover.

> **TIP:** I used a matching thread for the quilting, but feel free to experiment with different colors to add interest on this fun project!

### ASSEMBLING THE WEIGHT POCKETS

**1.** Fold each of the (4) 4″ squares of backing fabric in half on the diagonal and press. You now have four triangles.

**2.** Flip over the Quilted Cover so the backing fabric is facing up. Align one triangle with one corner of the cover, matching the raw edges of the triangle with the raw edges of the cover. Pin in place. (Fig. 6)

*Figure 6*

**3.** Repeat with the other three triangles in the remaining corners.

**4.** Use your sewing machine to attach the binding to the backing, ensuring that you catch the four Triangle Pockets in your stitching. Fold over the binding to the right side of the Quilter Cover (encasing the raw edges). Hand stitch binding closed.

**5.** Place weights in each of the Triangle Pockets and hand stitch each one closed.

*Plum*
PUDDING

ircles are one of my favorite shapes when it comes to just about anything. They have many meanings, such as totality, completeness and infinity. Wouldn't this be a fabulous quilt to give as a wedding present to celebrate the union of two individuals or as a 50-year anniversary quilt to your grandparents? This has become one of my favorite quilts to create, and design.

**Finished Quilt Size:**
72" x 72"

**Finished Block Size:**
12" x 12"

## Materials
**16 Assorted Purple Fabrics:** ¼ yard each

**12 Assorted White, Cream, or Low-Volume Fabrics:** ⅜ yard each, OR a total of 4½ yards

**Backing Fabric:** 4½ yards

**Binding Fabric:** ⅝ yards

**Batting:** 78" x 78"

**Fusible Web:** 7½ yards (based on a 20" width)

**Card stock or template plastic**

**Freezer paper (optional)**

## Preparation
Enlarge and cut out the Wedge Template (see page 76) and the Arc Template (see page 77) onto card stock or template plastic.

## Cutting
**From each Purple Fabric, cut:**

(1) 7" x WOF strip
  *Using the Wedge Template, Subcut 9 Wedges from each fabric, turning the template by 180 degrees every other cut, for a total of 144 Wedges*

**From the Assorted White, Cream, or Low-Volume Fabrics, cut:**
A total of (12) 12½" x WOF strips
  *Subcut into (3) 12½" squares, for a total of 36 squares*

**From Backing Fabric, cut:**
(2) 40" x 78" rectangles

**From Binding Fabric, cut:**
(8) 2½" x WOF strips

**From Fusible Web, cut:**
(18) 14½" x WOF rectangles

## Sewing the Arcs

**1.** Sew together 4 Wedge pieces along the long sides to create an arc. (Fig. 1)

*Figure 1*

**2.** Place Arc Template (see page 77) on top of the assembled unit from Step 1 and trim away excess fabric. (Fig. 2)

*Figure 2*

**3.** Repeat Steps 1-2 for a total of 36 Arcs.

> **TIP:** Try using freezer paper to create your Arc Template. When you place the template on the wedge unit, press lightly with an iron so that the template will stay in place temporarily while you trim around it.

**4.** Place 2 Arcs face down on a rectangle of fusible web. The textured side of the fusible web should be facing up. (Fig. 3)

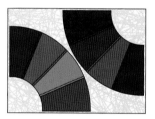

*Figure 3*

**5.** Trim the fusible web around each of the Arcs and set one aside.

**6.** Sew the Arc and web together using a ¼″ seam on both the inside and outside of the Arc (leaving the short ends open). Trim the fusible around the Arc, leaving at least a ⅛″ seam allowance.

**7.** Inside the seam allowance, clip the outer curve and notch the inner curve for give. This also decreases the chance of ripping the fusible web. Make sure you don't clip too closely — the stitch line must stay intact. (Fig. 4)

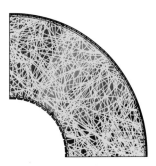

*Figure 4*

**8.** Carefully turn the Arc right side out. (Fig. 5)

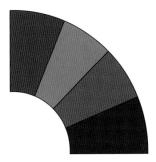

*Figure 5*

**9.** Gently push out the curve on the fabric side of the seam. This can be done with your fingernail, a pencil, or chopsticks. Finger press.

**10.** Repeat Steps 4-9 with the remaining Arcs to create a total of 36 Arc Appliqués.

## Assembling the Blocks

**1.** Fold each Background Square on the diagonal and press to create a crease.

**2.** Place the Arc Appliqué on top of a Background Square with the fusible web side facing down. Position so that the center seam of the Arc Appliqué aligns with the crease in the Background Square (Fig. 6). The raw edges of the arc and the background square should also align. Pin into place.

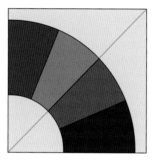

*Figure 6*

**3.** With your steam setting off and your iron on high, fuse the Arc Appliqué to the Background Square.

**4.** Repeat for a total of 36 blocks.

## Assembling the Quilt Top

**1.** Referencing Figure 7 and paying close attention to the placement of the arcs, lay out 6 rows of 6 blocks each.

**2.** Sew blocks together into rows, pressing seams to one side.

**3.** Sew rows together, pressing seams to one side.

## Finishing

**1.** Layer with batting and backing fabric, baste, and quilt as desired.

**2.** Attach binding using your favorite method.

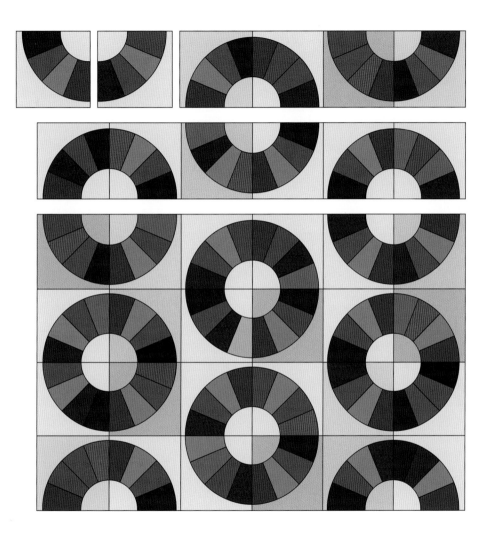

*Figure 7*

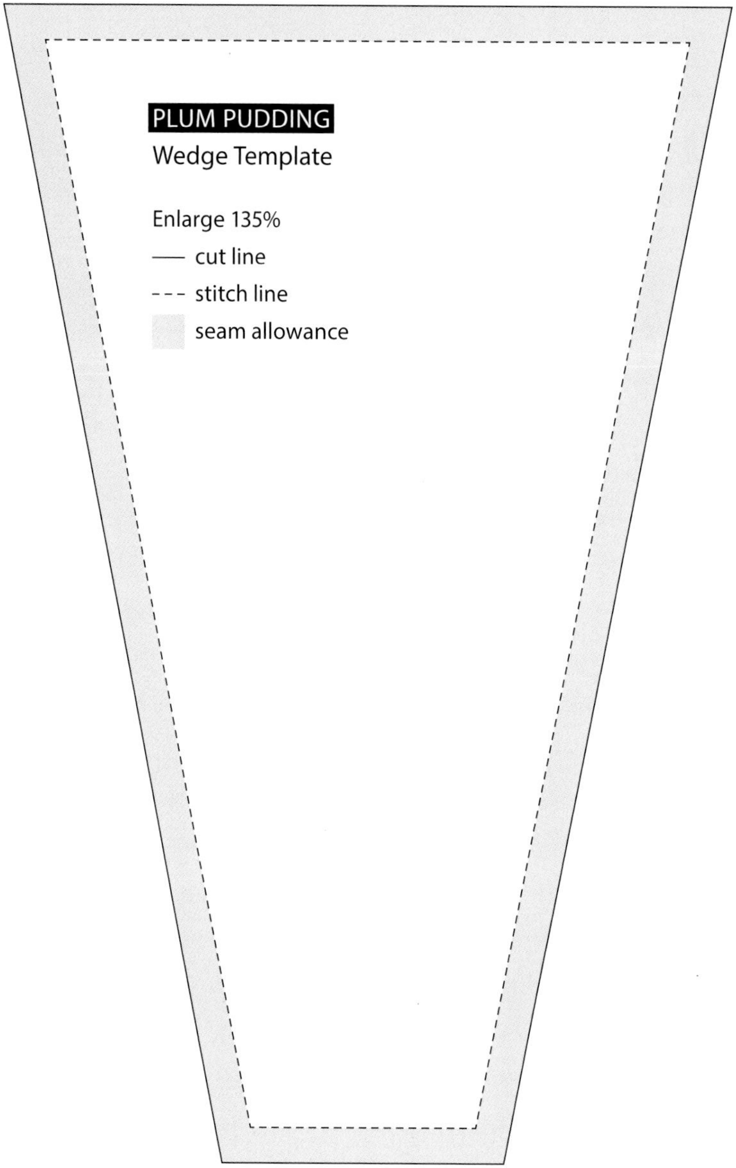

## PLUM PUDDING
Wedge Template

Enlarge 135%
— cut line
--- stitch line
seam allowance

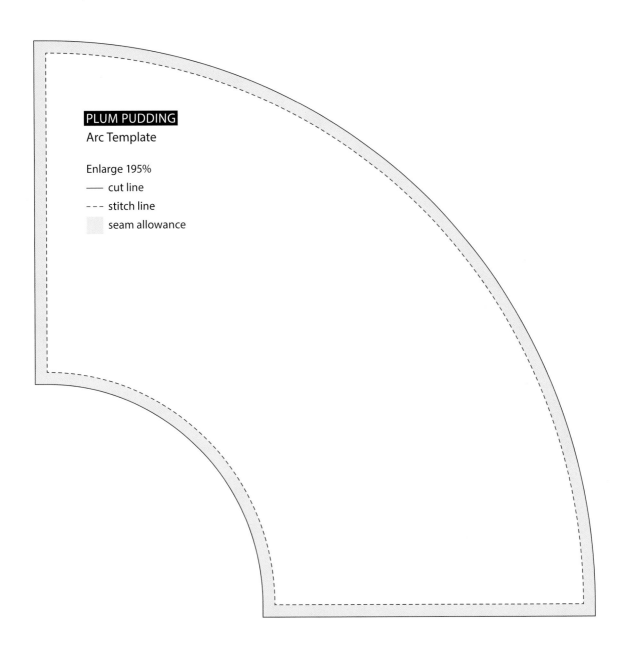

PLUM PUDDING
Arc Template

Enlarge 195%
—— cut line
--- stitch line
▨ seam allowance

*Cathedral Window*

# PLACE
# MATS

*I*'ve long been obsessed with the look of intricacy of cathedral window blocks. Ever since I learned how to make a cathedral window, I've loved the process. Sure to dress up any meal, these place mats will be a must have for your home, and a must make for housewarming gifts! If a full-size cathedral quilt is daunting, this place mat project will give you a taste and perhaps the confidence and love of making cathedral windows, enough to help you make that commitment to making a quilt!

**Finished Place Mat Size:**
approximately 19" x 14"

## *Materials (makes one place mat)*

**Tan Fabric:** 1 yard

**Purple Fabric Scraps:**
(17) 4¼" squares

**Binding Fabric:** ¼ yard

**Disappearing ink pen**

**Fabric glue stick**

## *Cutting*

**From Tan Fabric, cut:**
(3) 10" strips
  *Subcut (4) 10" squares from each strip*

**From Binding Fabric, cut:**
(2) 2½" strips

## Folding the Cathedral Window

**1.** On the right side of a Tan Square, mark a ¼″ seam all around the block. (I used a disappearing pen, but you can use a pencil — the markings will not be visible.)

**2.** Position the square so the wrong side is facing up. Fold in an edge using the ¼″ line as your guide. Press with an iron. Do this to each side of the square. (Fig. 1)

**3.** With wrong sides together, fold the square in half. Press to make a vertical line.

**4.** Unfold the square. With wrong sides together, fold along the horizontal axis. Press. When you unfold your square, the creases will divide it into quarters. (Fig. 2)

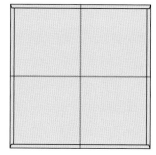

*Figure 2*

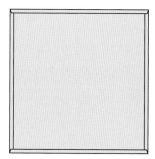

*Figure 1*

**5.** Fold in each corner toward the middle of the square. Press. (Fig. 3)

> **TIP:** You can use a regular glue stick or fabric glue stick to secure your folds so they won't shift around later on in the project. Just add a small dab near the corners to secure your first set of folds.

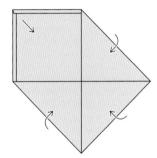

*Figure 3*

**6.** Repeat Step 5, folding the corners toward the middle of the square once more to make a Double-Folded Square. Take your time — the square will be double the thickness. Be sure to create sharp corners. Press.

**7.** Repeat Steps 1-6 to create a total of 12 Double-Folded Squares.

## Joining the Squares

**1.** Referring to Figure 4, arrange the 12 Double-Folded Squares in three rows of four squares.

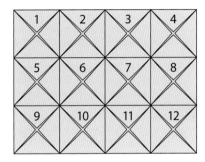

*Figure 4*

**2.** Lift the right flap on Square 1 and the left flap of Square 2, aligning the triangles (Fig. 5). Be sure the fold creases align and pin into place.

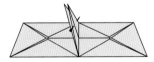

*Figure 5*

**3.** Repeat Step 2 for Squares 2/3 and 3/4, pinning together the first row.

**4.** Repeat Step 2 for Squares 5/6, 6/7, 7/8, pinning together the second row.

**5.** Repeat Step 2 for Squares 9/10, 10/11, 11/12, pinning together the third row.

**6.** Join the folded squares into rows by sewing along the creased lines on each pair of pinned triangles (Fig. 6). Each row will have a total of three seams.

**7.** Join the rows in a similar fashion, aligning the bottom creases in Row 1 with the top creases in Row 2. Sew together. Repeat to join Row 3. (Fig. 7)

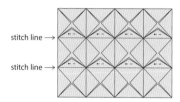

*Figure 7*

**8.** Be sure to fold the outer flaps back in.

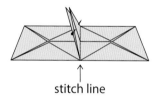

stitch line

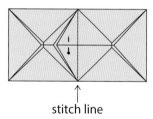

stitch line

*Figure 6*

**9.** Using a backstitch, sew a small X at each junction of four folded corners. This will hold the folds in place and help create smooth, even curves. (Fig. 8)

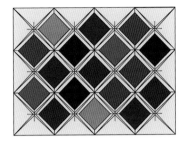

*Figure 9*

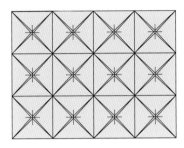

*Figure 8*

**10.** Place the Purple Squares in the open square areas of the 12-Block Unit. Dab a small amount of glue from your glue stick on the back of each of the 4¼" Purple Squares as you center them. (Fig. 9)

**11.** Gently fold in the loose folds to cover the raw edges of your Purple Squares. Pin into place (see photo on page 86).

**12.** Gently fold in the loose folds toward the empty blocks along the outer edges. Pin into place.

## CREATING CATHEDRAL WINDOWS

Cathedral Windows look difficult to make, but the folding and pressing make these arcs surprisingly simple to create. Here are some tips to make the process go more smoothly:

- Use the finest (thinnest) pins you can find.

- Finger press the curves into place rather than using an iron.

- If you are a fan of starch, use it for keeping all the folds flat in the Folding the Cathedral Window section (see page 82).

- If you are machine-sewing the arcs into place, pin and sew a few windows at a time to reduce the weight of the place mat due to all those pins and reduce the chances of pricking yourself too.

- Try leaving some of the windows empty (not including a purple square in the middle) for a more modern look.

## Finishing

**1.** Hand- or machine-sew the arcs to secure them, being sure to go through all layers. Because this is a place mat, I chose to machine-stitch the arcs so that it can be easily machine-washed.

> **TIP:** When stitching the arcs into place, make sure you stay as close to the outer edge of the arc as you feel comfortable.

**2.** Attach binding using your favorite method.

# *Grape* JUICE

sing paper piecing gives you the exactness you desire on all your points! This design gives the illusion of circles being chained together. A great throw quilt to nestle under while watching a movie, eating popcorn and sipping a drink.

## Cutting

**From Background Fabric, cut:**

(40) 3½'' x WOF strips

  *Subcut (6) 3½'' x 6½'' rectangles from each strip, for a total of 240 rectangles*

**From Pink Fabric, cut:**

(17) 5'' x WOF strips

  *from (8) strips, Subcut (30) 5'' x 9'' rectangles*

  *from (6) strips, Subcut (30) 5'' x 7'' rectangles*

  *from (3) strips, Subcut (30) 5'' x 3'' rectangles*

**From Purple Fabric, cut:**

(17) 5'' x WOF strips

  *from (8) strips, Subcut (30) 5'' x 9'' rectangles*

  *from (6) strips, Subcut (30) 5'' x 7'' rectangles*

  *from (3) strips, Subcut (30) 5'' x 3'' rectangles*

**From Backing Fabric, cut:**

(2) 33½'' x 78'' rectangles

**From Binding Fabric, cut:**

(7) 2½'' x WOF strips

## PAPER PIECING

**1.** To make a template, draw a 6½" square on a piece of 20 lb. paper. Center a 6" square inside that. From the lower left corner of the inner square, draw 4 lines using Figure 1 as a reference. Number each section. (Fig. 1)

**2.** Cut your fabric a little bigger than you normally would for machine piecing. Beginning with Section 1, pin your fabric to the wrong side of the template, leaving at least ¼" of fabric extending past the drawn lines. The right side of the fabric should be facing up. (Fig. 2)

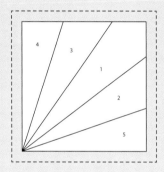

*Figure 1*

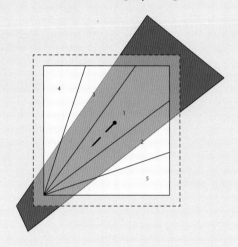

*Figure 2*

**3.** After ensuring that your fabric selection for Section 2 also has at least ¼" around all sides (hold the layers up to a sunny window to check), place fabric for Section 2 on top of fabric for Section 1, right sides together. Pin in place if needed. Flip over your template so that the numbers are facing you and the fabric is on the bottom.

**4.** Set your machine's stitch length to 1.5 mm. This will make removing the template paper a lot easier. Sew along the line between Sections 1 and 2, extending into the seam allowance.

**5.** Fold the paper along the sewn line so that the right side of Section 2 is on top of the right side of Section 1. Do not unfold the fabric. Use a ruler to measure ¼" away from the sewn

line onto the exposed fabric. Trim the excess fabric with a rotary cutter. Flip over the template and press the fabric open.

**6.** Repeat for all sections of the template, working in numerical order. (Fig. 3)

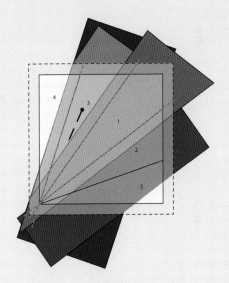

*Figure 3*

**7.** Press all seams again, this time on the right side of the fabric. (Fig. 4)

**8.** With the paper side facing up, trim around the template. Make sure to include any marked seam allowances. (Fig. 5)

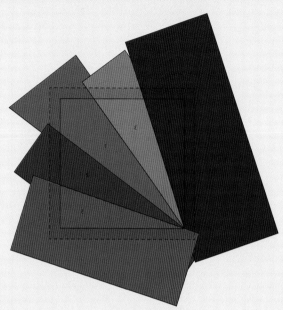

*Figure 4*

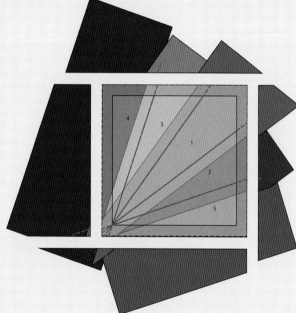

*Figure 5*

You did it! If you are working on a larger project with many paper-pieced components, you may want to wait until the top is completely assembled before removing the paper. If not, carefully remove the paper from the back, being sure not to distort the shape of the block.

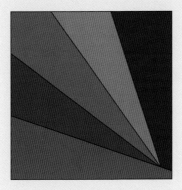

## Preparation

**1.** If paper piecing is new to you or if you need a refresher, try the practice block on page 92 before piecing the Grape Juice Blocks.

**2.** There are 2 finished blocks for this project, each with 4 paper-pieced units. I recommend piecing one unit at a time to minimize confusion regarding fabric placement.

**3.** Make 60 copies of Template A and 60 copies of Template B (see pages 104 and 105).

> **TIP:** Use a glue stick to tack down the fabric to the section you are paper piecing to make sure your fabric doesn't shift.

## Paper Piecing the Blocks

**PURPLE-DOMINANT BLOCK**

**1.** Referencing Figure 1 for fabric placement, position Section 1 on Template A with the Background Fabric and paper wrong sides together.

**2.** Continue to paper piece the remaining sections of Template A with the Purple Fabric in Section 2 and the Background Fabric in Section 3. (Fig. 1)

**3.** Repeat to create a total of 30 Purple A Units.

*Figure 1: Make 30 A Units*

**4.** Referencing Figure 2 for fabric placement, position Section 1 on paper piecing Template B with the Background Fabric and paper wrong sides together.

**5.** Continue to paper piece the remaining sections of Template B with the Pink Fabric in Section 2, the Background Fabric in Section 3, and the Purple Fabric in Section 4. (Fig. 2)

**6.** Repeat to create a total of 30 Pink/Purple B Units.

*Figure 2: Make 30 B Units*

**7.** Gather 2 Unit As and 2 Unit Bs. Lay out units in a 4-Patch: (Row 1) A, B ; (Row 2) B, A. The purple corners should all meet in the center. (Fig. 3)

**8.** Sew blocks into rows. Press seams open.

**9.** Sew rows into the 4-patch. Press seams open. You may remove the paper here if you like, or wait until the entire top is put together.

**10.** Repeat Steps 7-9 to create a total of 30 Purple-Dominant Blocks.

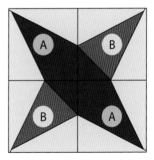

*Figure 3*

## PINK-DOMINANT BLOCK

**1.** Referencing Figure 4 for fabric placement, position Section 1 on Template A with the background fabric and paper wrong sides together.

**2.** Continue to paper piece the remaining sections of Template A with the Pink fabric in Section 2 and the background fabric in Section 3.

**3.** Repeat to create a total of 30 Pink A Units.

**4.** Referencing Figure 5 for fabric placement, position Section 1 on paper piecing Template B with the Background Fabric and paper wrong sides together.

**5.** Continue to paper piece the remaining sections of Template B with the Purple Fabric in Section 2, the Background Fabric in Section 3, and the Pink Fabric in section 4.

**6.** Repeat to create a total of 30 Purple/Pink B Units.

*Figure 4: Make 30*

*Figure 5: Make 30*

**7.** Gather 2 Unit As and 2 Unit Bs. Lay out units in a 4-Patch: (Row 1) A, B ; (Row 2) B, A. The pink corners should all meet in the center. (Fig. 6)

**8.** Sew blocks into rows. Press seams open.

**9.** Sew rows into the 4-Patch. Press seams open. You may remove the paper here if you like, or wait until the entire top is put together.

**10.** Repeat Steps 7-9 to create a total of 30 Pink-Dominant Blocks.

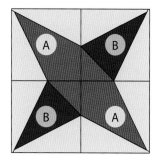

*Figure 6*

## Assembling the Rows

**1.** Referencing Figure 7, arrange the blocks into 6 rows of 5 blocks each.

**2.** Sew blocks together into rows. Press the seams to one side.

**3.** Sew rows together. Press, the seams to one side.

**4.** If you didn't remove your papers from the back of your blocks as you assembled them, remove them now.

> **TIP:** Use a rubber mallet to pound down bulky corners. In this project there are many points coming together and flattening these areas with the mallet will make it less bulky.

## Finishing

**1.** Layer with batting and backing fabric, baste, and quilt as desired.

**2.** Attach binding using your favorite method.

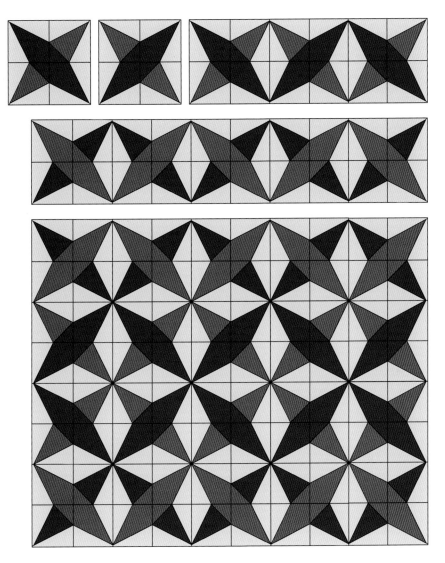

*Figure 7*

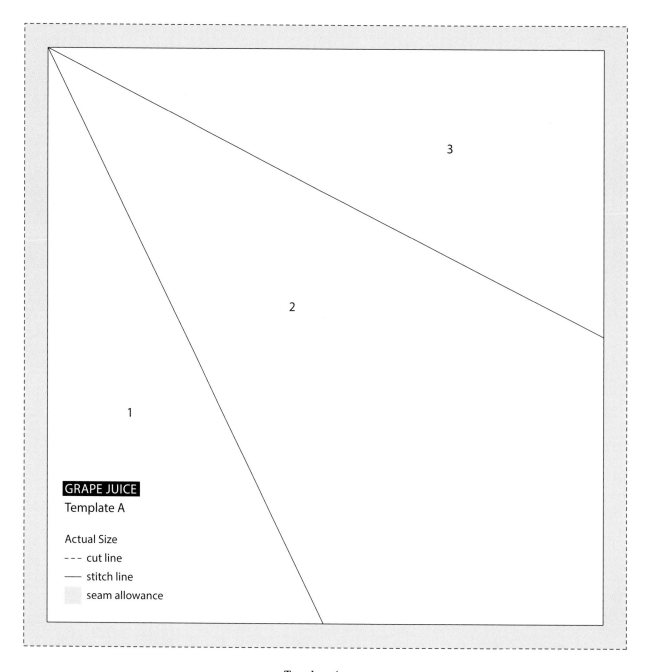

GRAPE JUICE
Template A

Actual Size
- - - cut line
—— stitch line
seam allowance

1

2

3

*Template A*

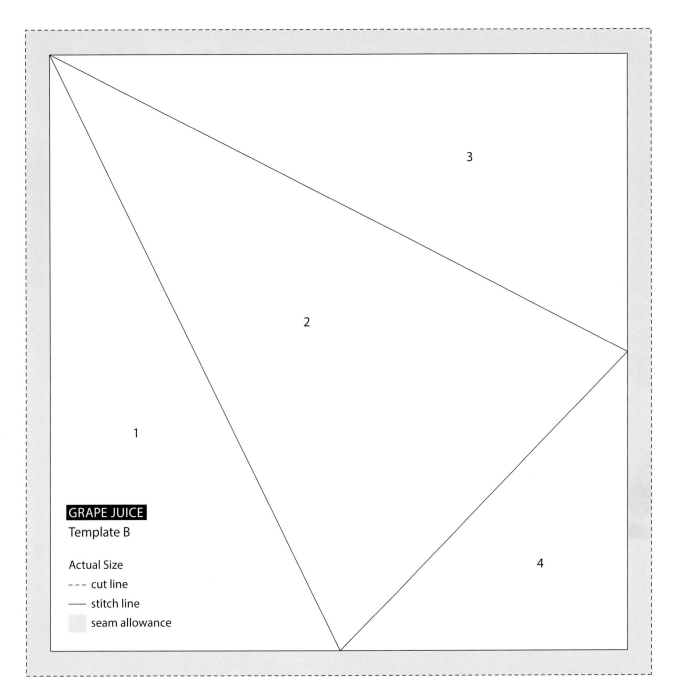

**Template B**

## ACKNOWLEDGMENTS

I am always in awe of the support and love my husband gives me. He's my biggest cheerleader, and best friend, and sometimes willing to give me the extra nudge I didn't even ask for to get me to push myself a little farther than I normally would. I'm eternally grateful for him and our children. They are my rock and the main reason that I am who I am and why I do what I do. Of course, there are a few great friends whom I've been able to bounce ideas off of and whom I asked to help me with sewing trial runs of projects. To each of them, I thank you from the bottom of my heart for your support and help. I would also like to thank Moda fabrics for supplying fabric for the projects in this book and for cheering me on from the get-go. Thank you also to Robert Kaufman, Andover, and Frond for supplying additional fabrics. Thank you to Sarah Gustason for her quilting expertise. Of course, thank you to Susanne Woods, for her drive, her talent, and her vision. I appreciate your insight and support of this project. I'm grateful for the Lucky Spool Media team that helped to polish and package the book into a beautiful work of art. I am so blessed both within and outside the quilting industry, and this book is a product of all the love and support I receive in my life.

# *My range of fabrics, threads and Simply Color books*

**Vanessa Christenson** is a blogger, quilter, and pattern designer who is well-known for her original sense of style and unique take on traditional motifs. Vanessa began blogging while her husband was deployed as a means of keeping in touch, but it wasn't long before others started to take notice of the projects she was making. One of the first opportunities offered to her was to participate as a Chef for the Moda Bake Shop website, sponsored by Moda Fabrics. Since then, her designs have been featured in numerous magazines, including: Stitch Magazine, Quilty Magazine, Quilts and More, and Fons and Porter's Love of Quilting. She is the author of the highly rated book Make it Sew Modern and has contributed quilt designs to numerous compilation books. Vanessa is an in-demand public speaker and has also been featured on television and web based media outlets, such as: Quilting Arts with Pokey Bolton, Fons and Porter: Love of Quilting, and Craftsy. Over the years, Vanessa's relationship with Moda Fabrics continued to grow and it was through them that she released

her wildly successful first fabric line and Aurifil thread collection, Simply Color, in 2012. She recently released her fourth fabric line and there are more on the way. In addition to all of her other activities, Vanessa is also a BERNINA Ambassador and contributor to the We All Sew blog sponsored by BERNINA. Although she has found immense success in quilting, fabrics, and pattern design, Vanessa is quick to point out that her most important role is as a wife and as a mother to their four children. Vanessa's designs, projects, and patterns can be found on her website, www.vchristenson.com.